BASIC PENKNIFE CARVING

with Tom Wolfe

Text written with and photography by Douglas Congdon-Martin

Schiffer Publishing Ltd

77 Lower Valley Road, Atglen, PA 19310

Published by Schiffer Publishing, Ltd.
77 Lower Valley Road
Atglen, PA 19310
Please write for a free catalog.
This book may be purchased from the publisher.
Please include $2.95 postage.
Try your bookstore first.

We are interested in hearing from authors
with book ideas on related subjects.

Printed in the United States of America.
ISBN: 0-88740-499-5

Contents

Introduction

In some ways penknife carving is the purest form of the art. It isn't fancy or hard. The carver, the wood, and the knife combine to create something out of nothing. In the country we call this whittling, and many a relaxed afternoon is spent on the porch or in the shade of some old tree creating wood chips and miracles.

Where I come from no one would leave his house without a penknife in his pocket. They would be undressed. You never know when you'll need it either for some practical purpose, for keeping your hands busy while talking with friends, or for filling that creative urge.

The pattern we carve in this book is the first one I ever made. It was in the 8th grade and I was fixing to enter an art contest, and this was what I was going to do. But my teacher talked me out of making it, saying it was too hard. Maybe she was right, maybe not, but it was probably for the best since I didn't have a bandsaw anyway. Instead I entered a pastel drawing of a skyline of a hill in my hometown, called "A Strawberry Sunset." It showed the setting sun playing on the houses along the top of the hill. I won a gold key for my efforts, but my first love was still woodcarving.

I carved boats and rockets and other things, using bass wood and razor type knives. Gradually I got good enough to do things like the project in this book and more.

This book is woodcarving at its most basic. By learning to carve with one knife, you increase the skill you have and get ready to move on to more complex and creative work.

I hope you enjoy this book and that penknife carving will bring you the hours of entertainment it has brought me through the years.

The Reclining Figure

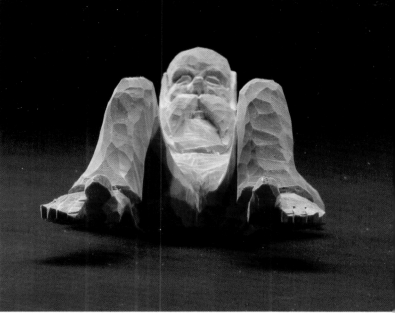
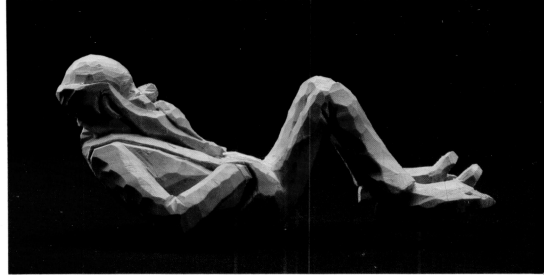
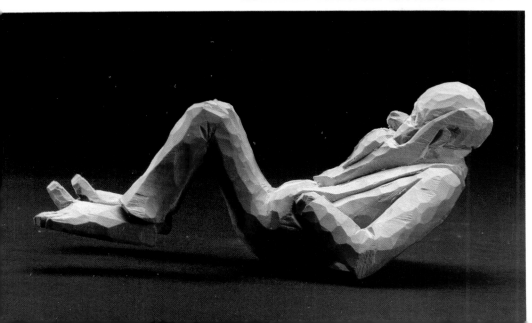

Carving the Reclining Figure

Cut the blank with a coping saw or bandsaw. The grain should run horizontally from foot to head.

Draw in the frontal details and mark the areas to be removed.

Resaw the piece to remove the excess. This should be done in two positions. On a bandsaw the lower body should be cut with the piece sitting upright, creating a vertical cut, and the head and shoulders should be cut with the figure laying on its back.

Draw in the center line from head to foot in the front.

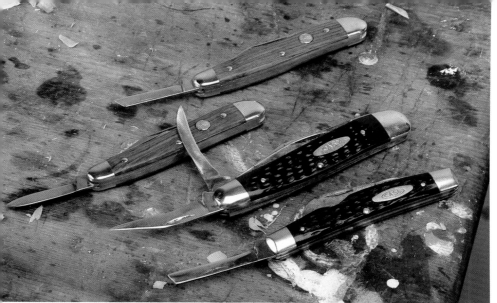

The top two knives are identical new knives with different blades showing. They also have a third, larger blade, which I seldom use. The next knife is my old whittler, with its blades ground down to my personal taste. The bottom knife is a four-bladed sway back pocket knife with a carpenter's blade showing. The key to a good whittling knife are good narrow blades.

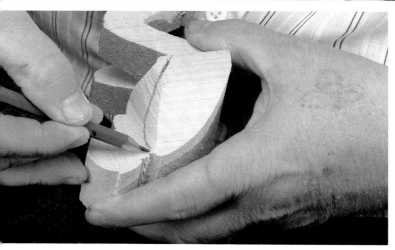

Draw in the shoulder lines on each side.

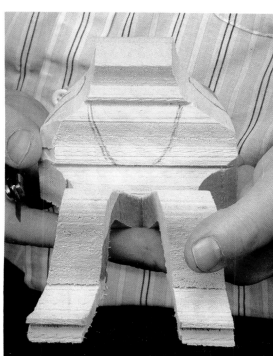

Draw in the beard line.

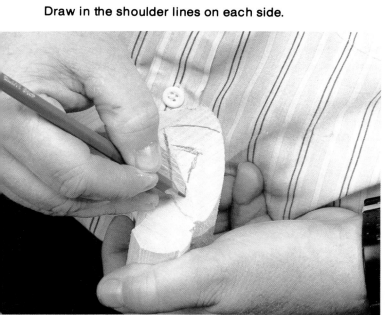

Also draw in the lines for the arms. Photos with the patterns can be used to make a pattern for tracing. Simply photocopy them to match the size of your carving. Make several copies.

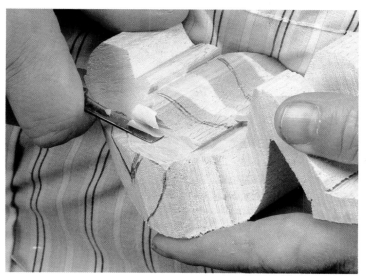

Trim away the area in front of the arm.

To bring out the head, cut straight down with the grain...

and trim back to it along the chest. Repeat the process until the head is the width you desire.

The head defined.

Knock the corners from the head. I always like to take my carvings to an octagonal shape before I round them off. This helps me avoid the common mistake of making the head too flat.

Continue by knocking off the corners of the beard.

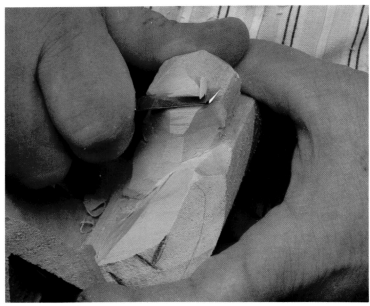

Round off the top of his head.

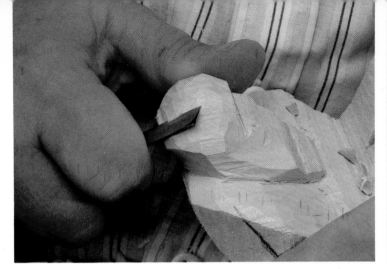

To get the roundness of our friend's bald head, keep moving around so you don't take off too much in one place.

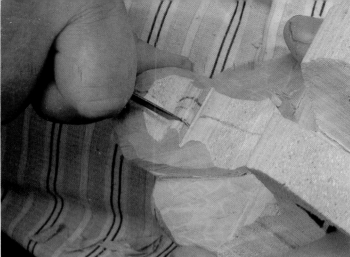

Make a stop on each side of the nose.

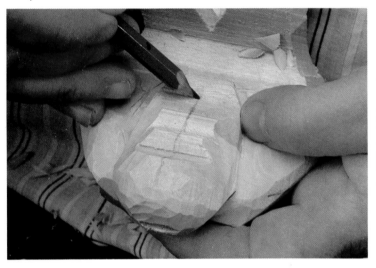

Mark the center line of the face to help keep the carving symmetrical.

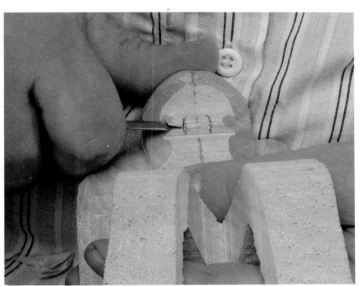

Come up beside the nose to remove the excess.

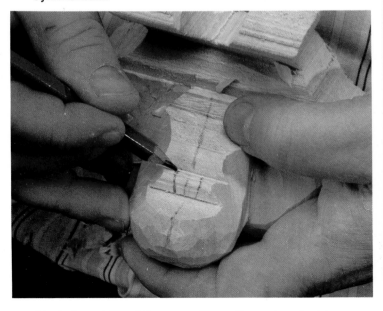

Mark the width of the nose. Keep it good and wide.

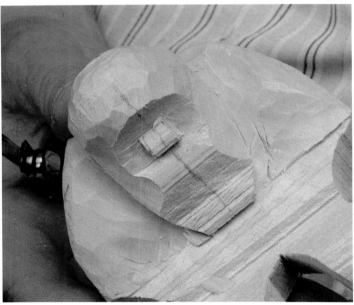

This results in a blocked-off nose.

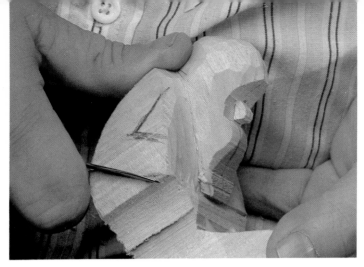

I want to leave the face for a while and round off some of the sharp edges. I begin with the lower arm. Make a stop on the line of the forearm. Rock your knife back and forth to get it deeper.

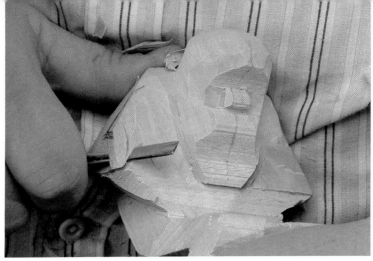

Trim away the corner of the upper arm to the shoulder.

Cut back to the stop from the hip. You can repeat the stop and trim method down to the hip.

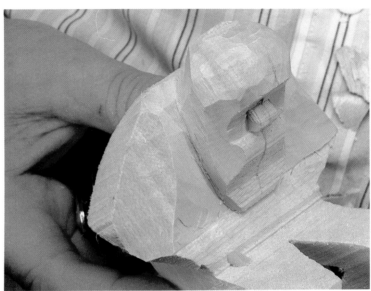

This is the result you are after.

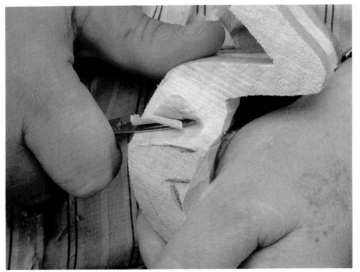

If the grain runs the right way, you can scoop the excess wood away.

Mark the big toes and the areas to be removed. The big toes will stick right up in the air.

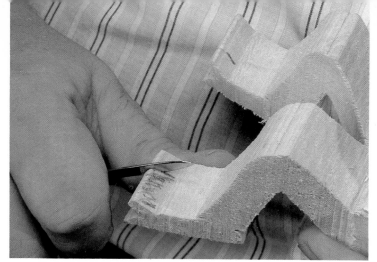

Cut a stop in the line....

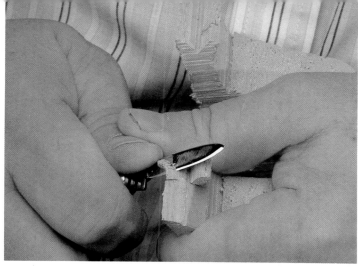

and trim back to it from under the toe, leaving the other four toes on the ground.

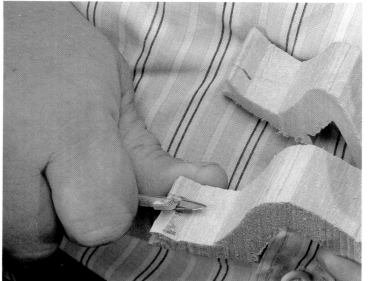

and trim back to it.

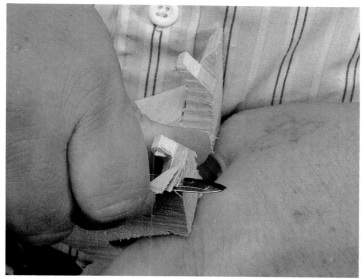

Round the four toes from the outside.

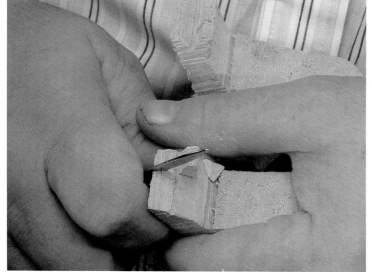

The same method is used in reverse under the big toe. Make a stop cut...

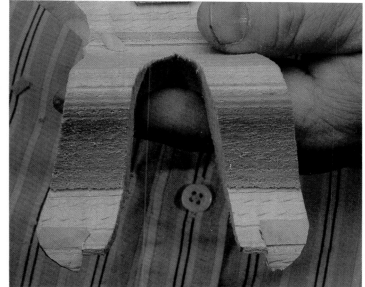

This gives you the graduated sizes you want for the toes.

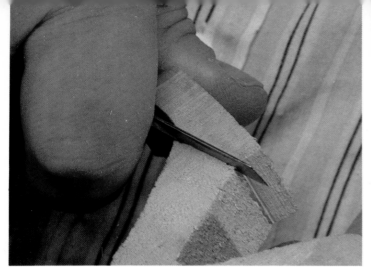

Cut a stop in the bottom of the pants.

Trim back to it from the foot.

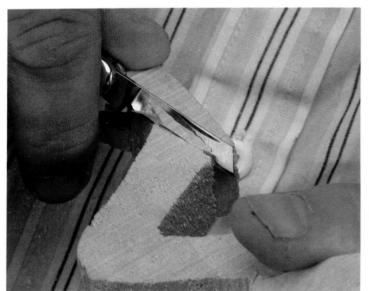

Trim back to it from the foot.

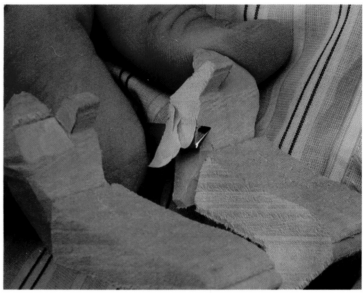

Shape the overall foot, making it smaller in the back than the front, and scooping out the instep.

Repeat the cut on the inside of the pants.

The basic shapes are established.

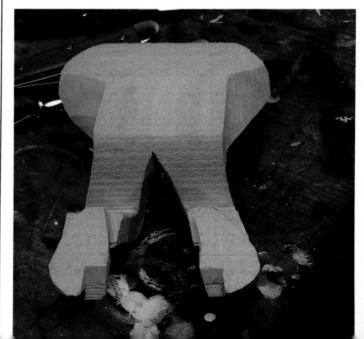

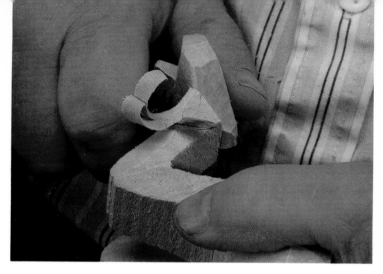

Starting with the legs, knock the corners off to get them to an octagonal shape.

You can see the flatness in the upper thigh. Since you can't add width...

Continue on the hip and the backside of the legs. I've noticed that my legs are not quite square enough. I need to fix it or they will look flat.

you need to narrow them down. In fact, this country figure needs to have pencil thin legs anyway, so it's not really a problem.

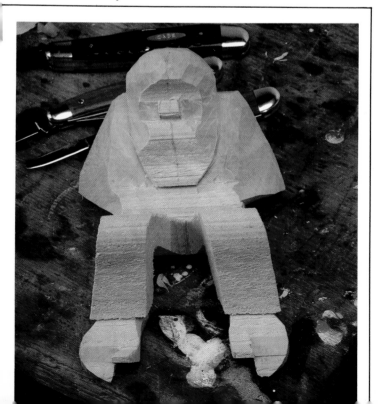

To keep things looking natural you will probably have to thin the hips a little bit too.

With the size set, begin to round the octagonal legs into round.

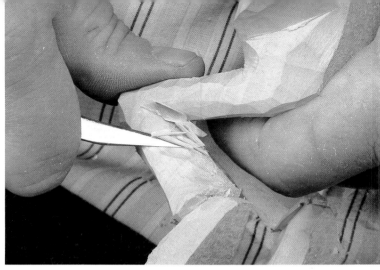

make some folds in the pants.

Round the lower leg, leaving a flare in the bottom of the pants.

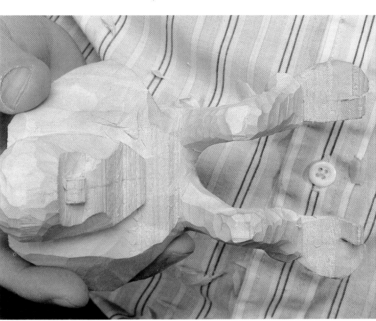

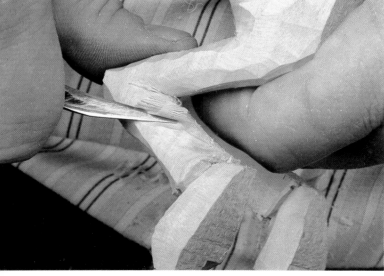

With a curl cut...

The legs so far.

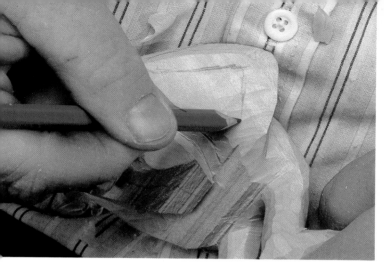

Mark the inside of the arm.

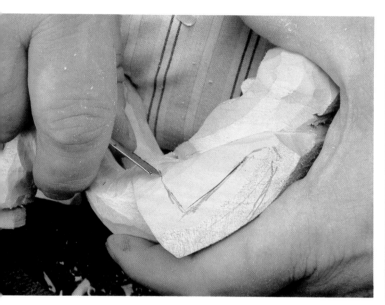

Cut a stop along the line of the arm.

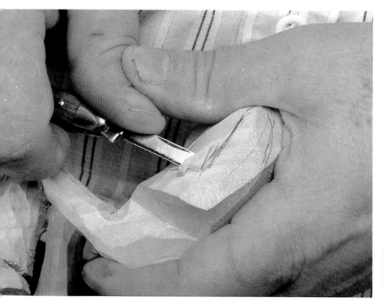

Trim back to it from the chest.

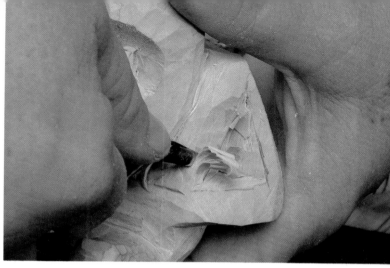

Repeat the stop and trim method until you get to the shape of the chest. The hands will be inside the bib overalls, which, of course, is the main reason people wear bib overalls.

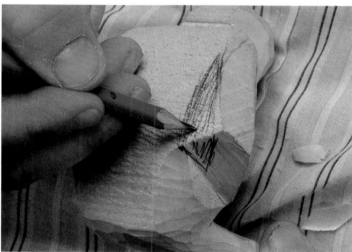

Turn to the back and mark the area to be removed between the elbow and the body. We want to go all the way through to the other side.

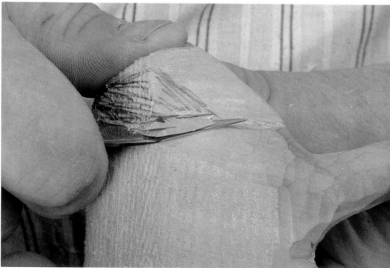

Cut out the area by slicing along the body...

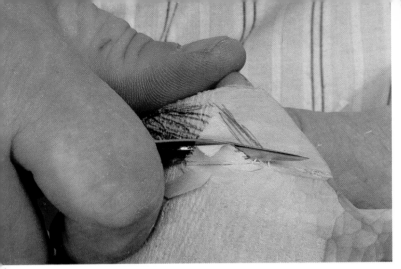

and cutting back to it.

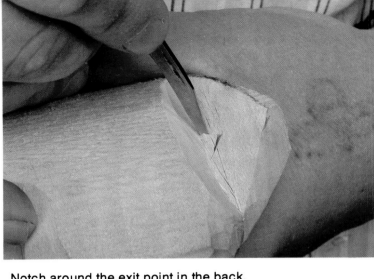

Notch around the exit point in the back.

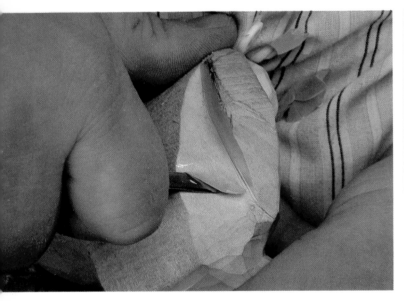

As you get deeper, skinny down the body a little.

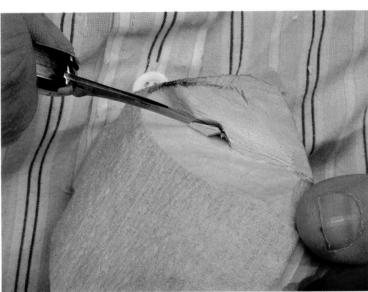

Once you establish the hole, it is just a matter of widening it. Whenever you can make an appropriate hole in a piece, it improves the quality of the carving/sculpture, giving it more depth and character.

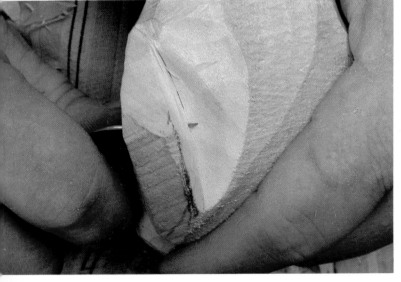

To get the line of the opening stick your knife through from front to back.

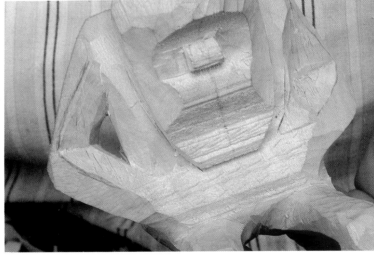

Trim the body and arm to blend with the hole.

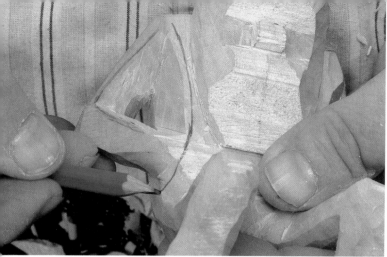

Draw in the line of the overalls.

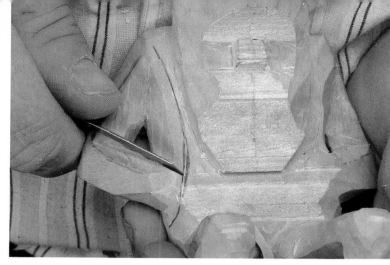

Cut a stop along the top line of the hand...

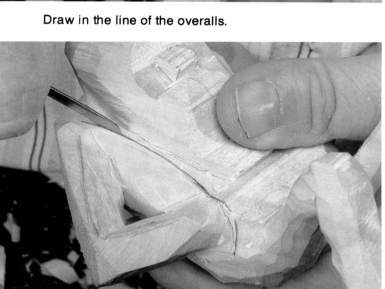

Cut a stop in the line.

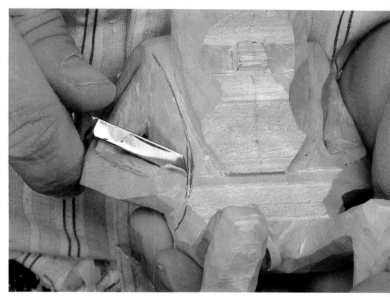

and cut back to it from the shirt. This makes the hand appear to go under the overall.

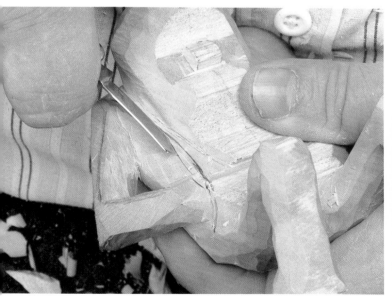

Slice back to it from the shirt and hand.

The head and shoulders are too wide, and the shoulders may be too hunched.

I draw in the narrowed lines of the head...

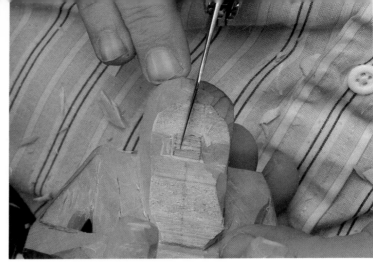

The narrowing has left the nose a little off center, so we need to trim one side. This was the whole reason of leaving the nose wide at the beginning. Cut a stop...

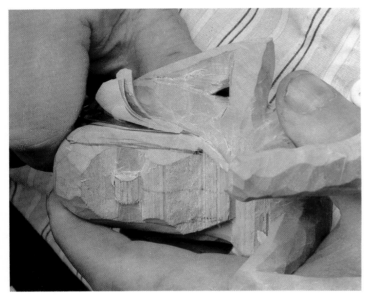

and trim it down. First I take several slices with the grain.

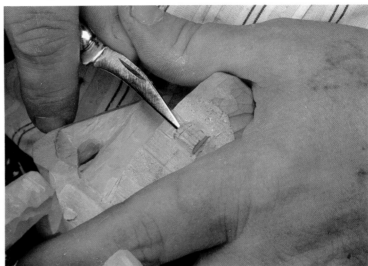

and cut down beside the nose.

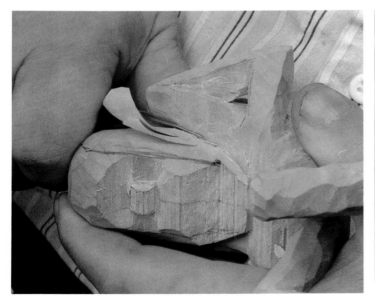

Then I go back and cut them off at the chest.

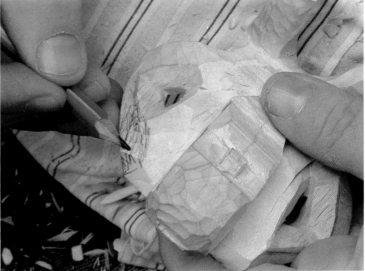

To narrow the shoulder I'll trim the upper arm. It's helpful to mark the area to be removed.

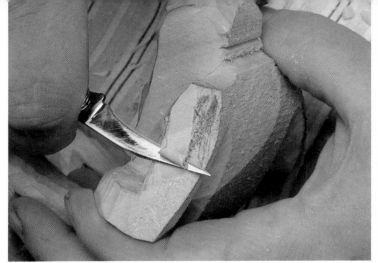

Slice off the excess.

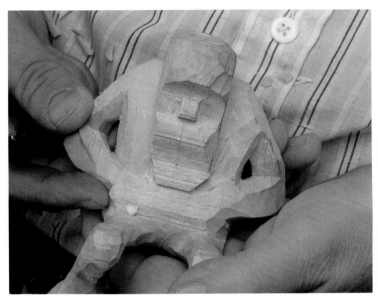

This thinning of the shoulders has reduced the "hunched" look of the shoulders.

Bring the chest into the new proportions.

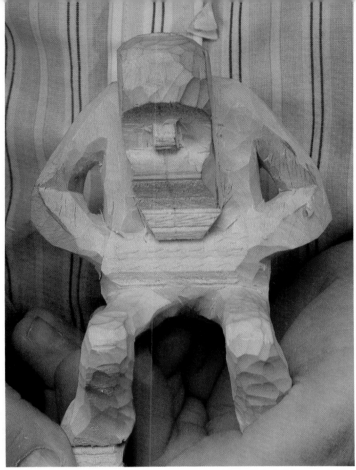

Now we're ready to shape the arms.

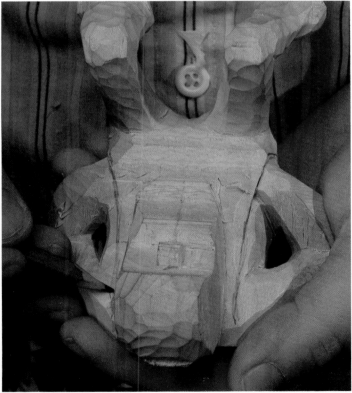

First redraw the overall bib and straps so you remember to leave room for them.

To shape the arms, begin by squaring them up. This will help you get the right proportions and the roundness you are after.

Draw in the back of the overalls.

The squared up arms give a good perspective for checking size and symmetry.

Knock the corners off the face.

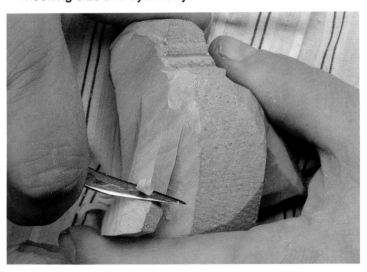

Take the arms to octagon shape by knocking off the corners.

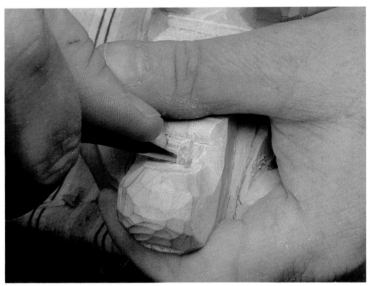

Knock the corners off the nose.

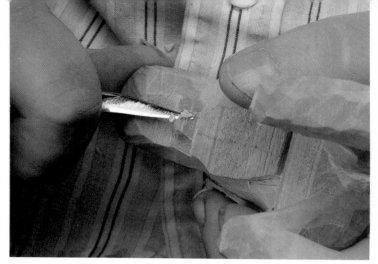

Continue to round the nose.

Create the bridge by cutting in at angle toward the top of the nose...

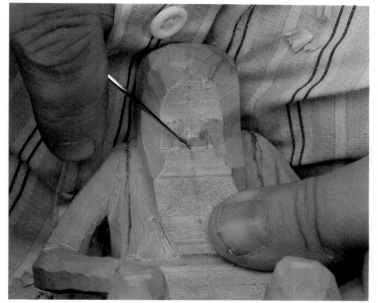

At the nostrils, cut in at a 45 degree angle...

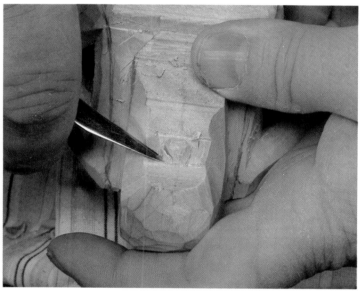

and trimming it off from the cheek.

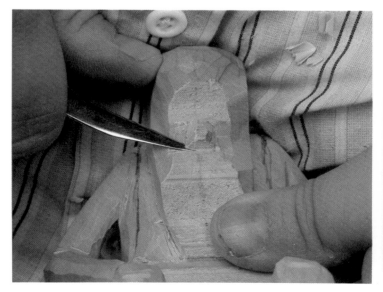

and come back and pick up the nitch.

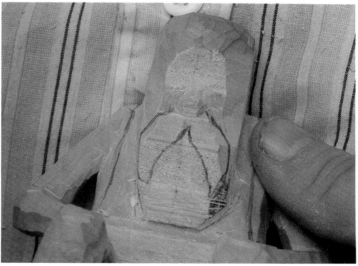

I think I want a big droopy moustache, but to be sure I always mark it off. I like it.

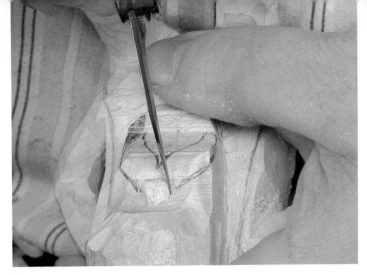

Cut a stop straight in beside the nose.

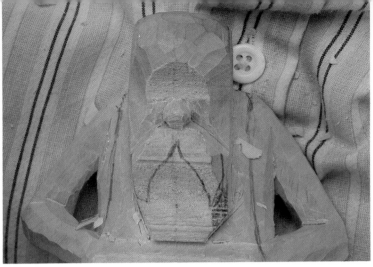

This gives you the top of the moustache and a little shape to the cheek.

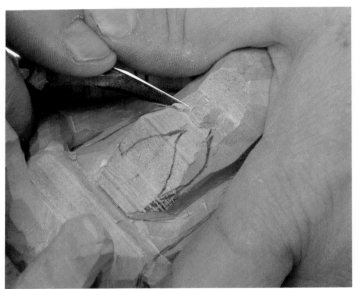

Then slice down the line of the cheek to the moustache.

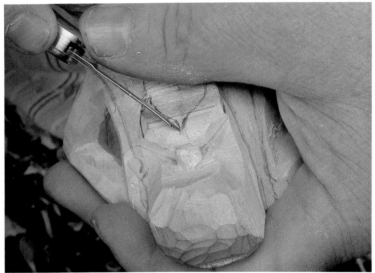

At the part of the moustache cut straight in one side...

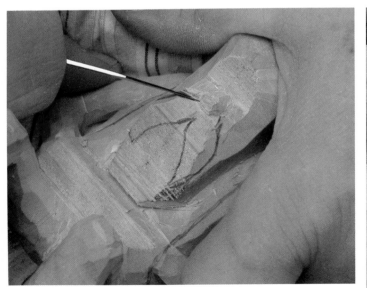

Cut in on the line of the moustache and a little triangle should pop out.

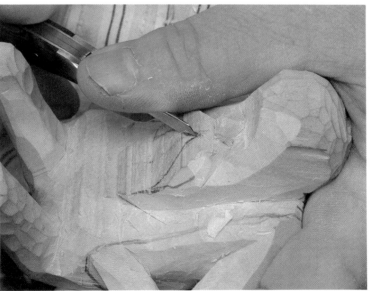

then the other.

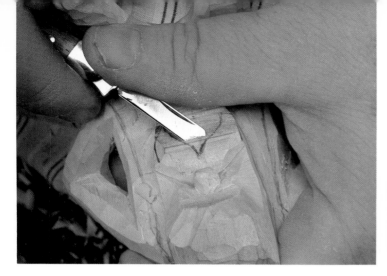

Come back to it from the bottom, forming the bottom edge of the moustache and the surface of the lower lip.

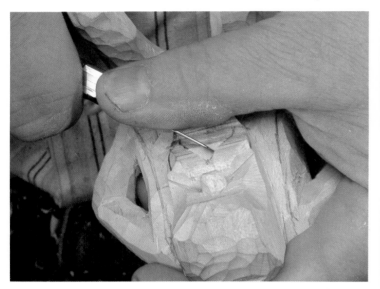

This same method is used lower down the carving to form the bottom of the lower lip. First cut an angle down and to the center.

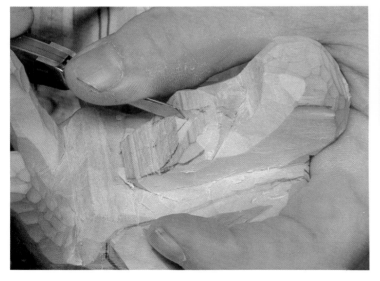

Then cut straight in along the moustache line.

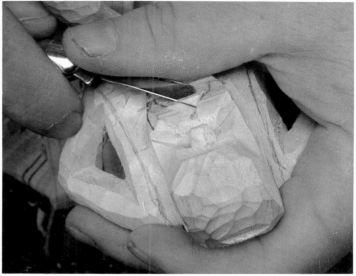

Clean the area in between following the surface of the beard.

Repeat on the other side of the moustache.

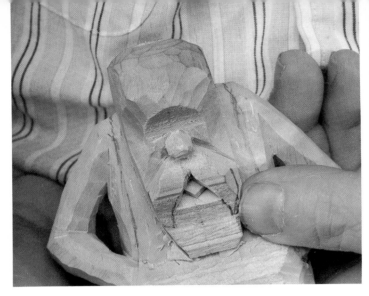

The result is a triangle that with some trimming will become the lip.

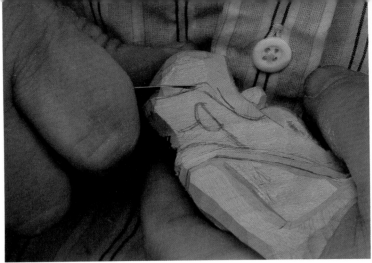

Trim back to it from the head...

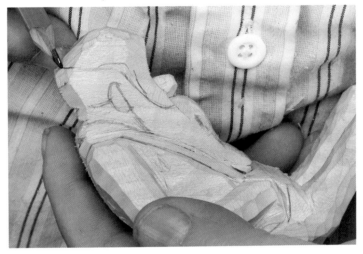

Starting at the hairline from the pattern at the back of the head, draw in the beard and ear details.

and face. Continue all the way around the hairline.

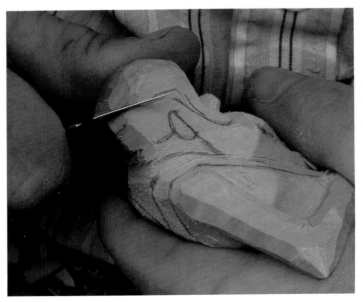

Cut a stop around the hair line.

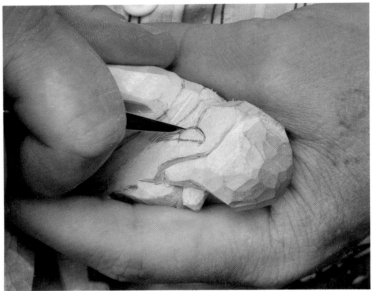

Cut a stop around the outside of the ear.

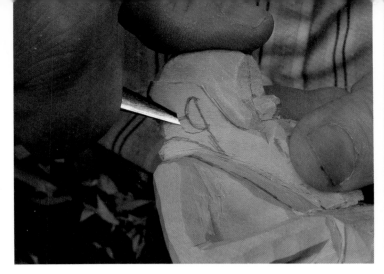

Cut a slice behind it, bringing the ear out.

Cut a stop at the bottom of the hairline.

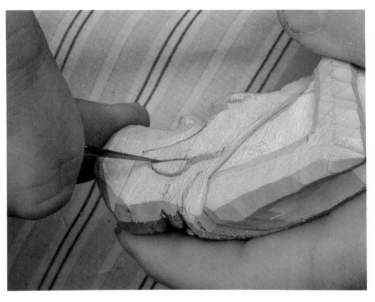

Cut a stop in front of the ear behind the sideburn.

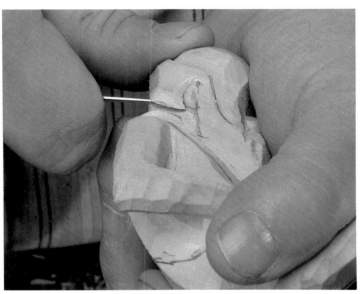

Trim back to it from the neck. Continue the process all around the head and neck.

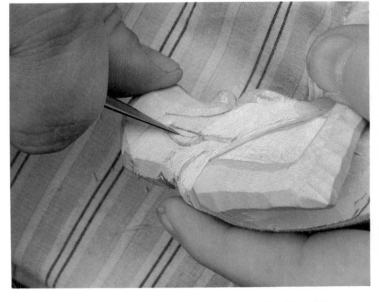

Use a curved angled cut to cup out the inside of the ear.

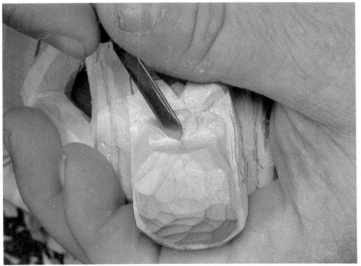

Angle a cut along the bridge of the nose using the point of the knife.

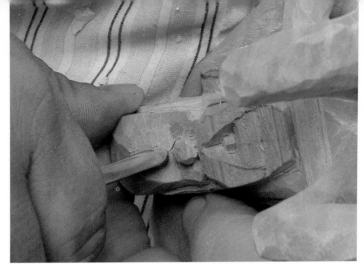

From the same point cut a line following the brow.

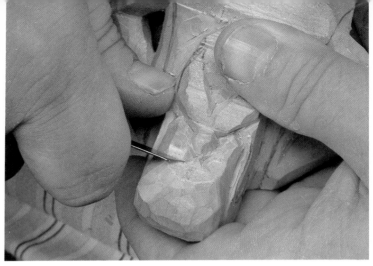

Repeat on the other side. Then cut straight in beneath the eyebrow.

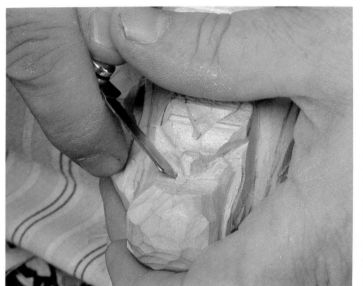

Make a slice into the triangle between those to lines.

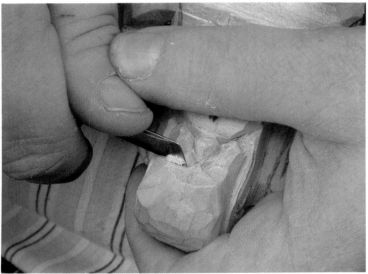

Cut back to it to leave the underside of the brow and the top of the eye.

This takes you to this point.

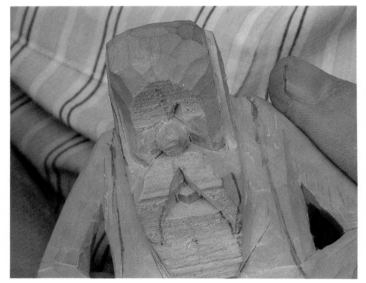

This defines the bridge of the nose and creates the inside corner of the eyesocket.

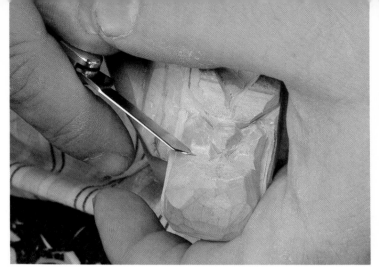

Continue the line to the outside of the eye cutting straight in....

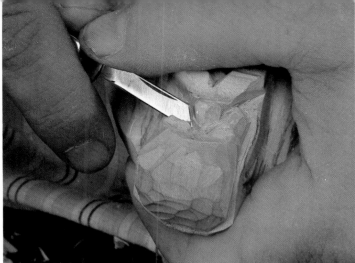

and cutting back to it.

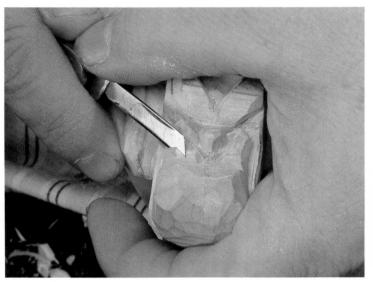

and back to it.

This gives a sleepy-eyed look.

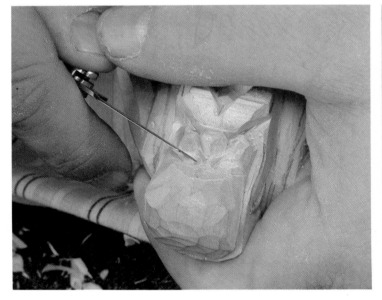

The eye is created by cutting straight in at an angle...

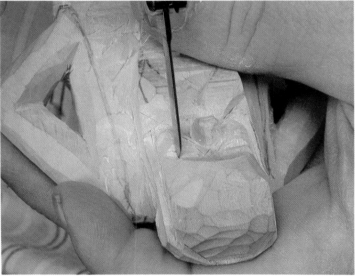

The eye is a little wide so I will bring it in from the outside. First make a stop at the width you want.

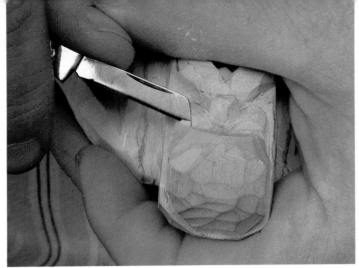

Then cut up along the stop.

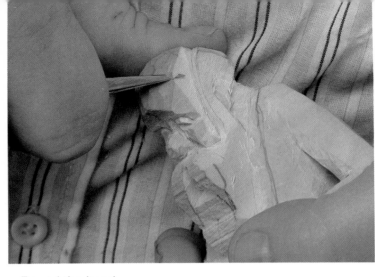

Round the head.

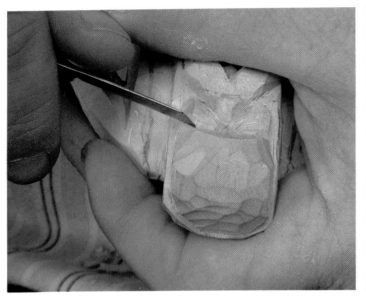

Finally trim back to it.

Continue refining the head.

This widens the area at the outside of the eye and narrows the eye.

Create the nostrils by sticking your knife straight in...

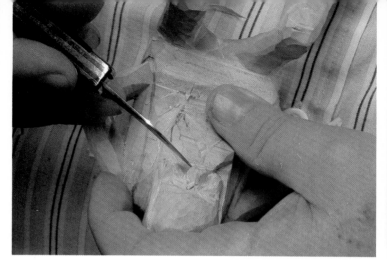

and then at a slight angle to form two sides of a small triangle.

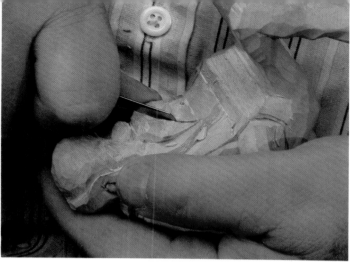

Cut stops on the moustache line...

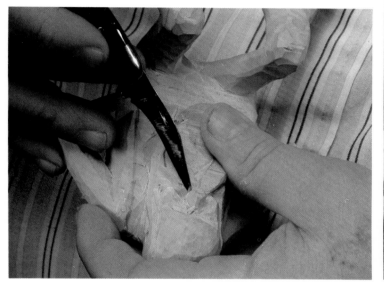

Come back on the third side of the triangle to pop out the nitch.

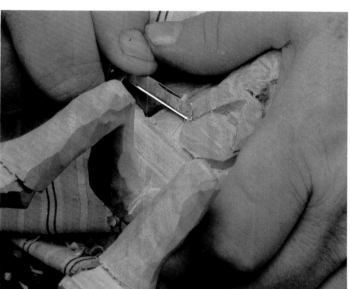

and slice beside them.

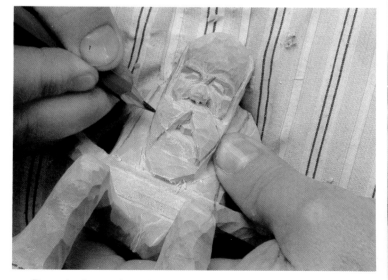

Draw in the walrus-like moustache. This will be the most dominant part of the face.

Progress on the head.

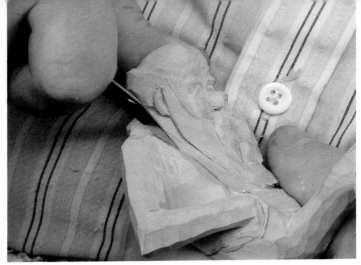

Cut a stop along the side of the overall bib....

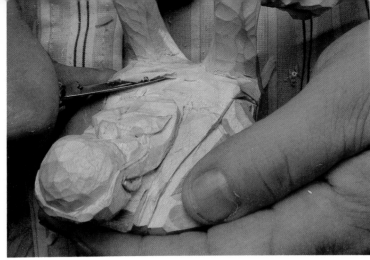

Refine and smooth the piece as problems catch your eye.

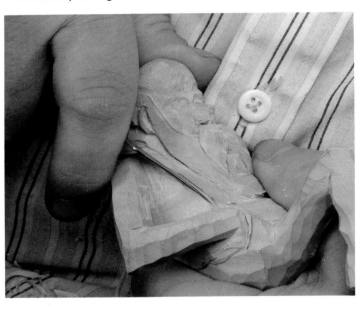

and trim back to it.

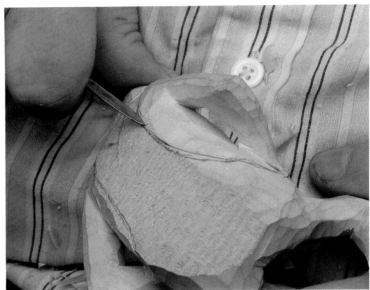

Carry the line of the overalls around the back in the same way: making a stop...

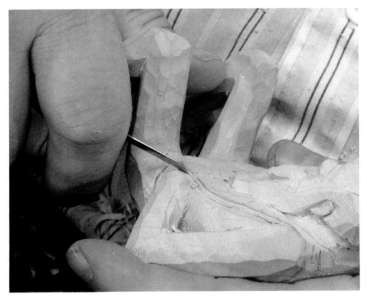

Continue the line over the hands.

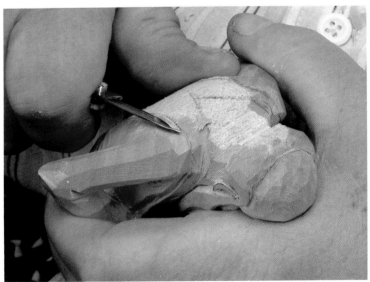

and trimming back to it.

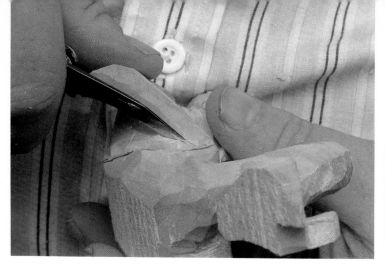

You want the hand to look like it is going under the overall, not blending into the body. Make a deep stop on the underside of the hand.

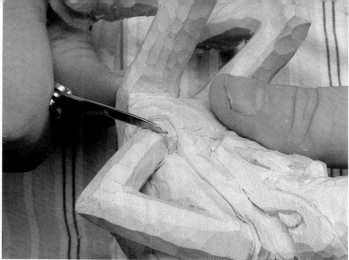

Cut a stop in it...

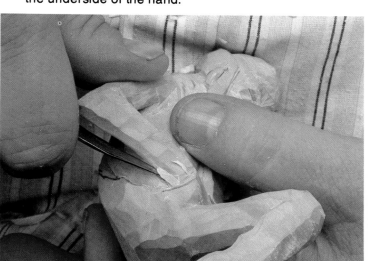

Trim back to it from below.

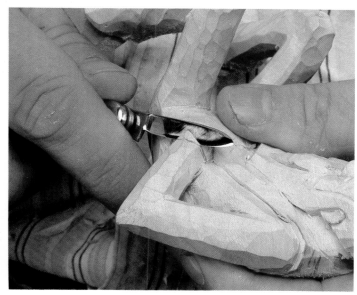

and trim back to it from the hand.

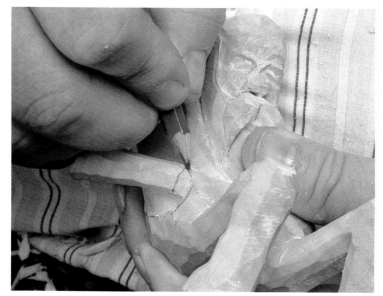

Draw the cuff of the sleeve.

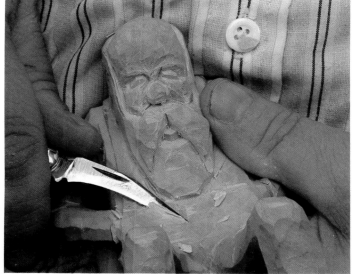

Trim a little groove in the overalls above the hand, so you can see the bulge the hand makes.

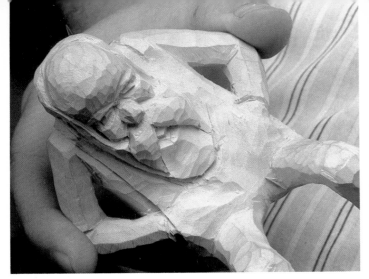

The result.

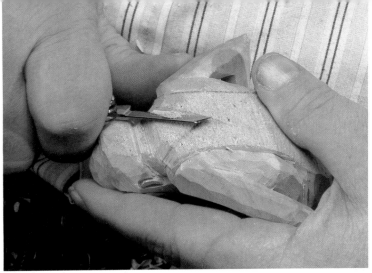

then shaving back to them.

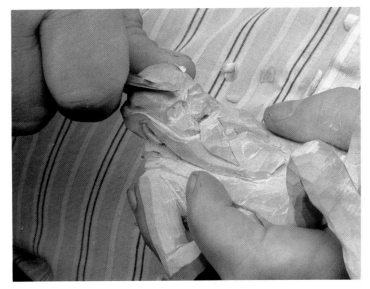

The forehead is a little prominent so I'll shave it down a bit.

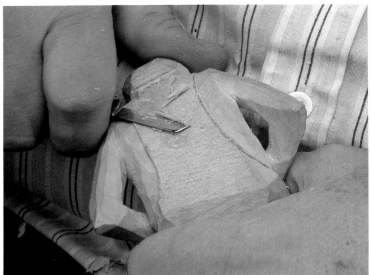

Clean the saw marks off the back of the overalls.

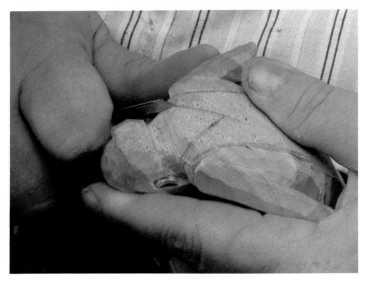

Clean up the V in the back of the overalls, first cutting stops in the lines...

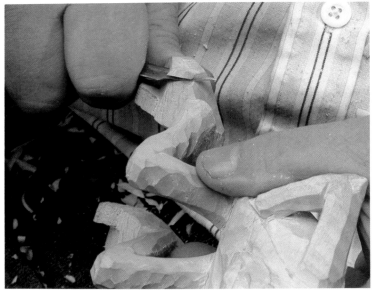

Bevel the front of the foot so it follows a natural toe line.

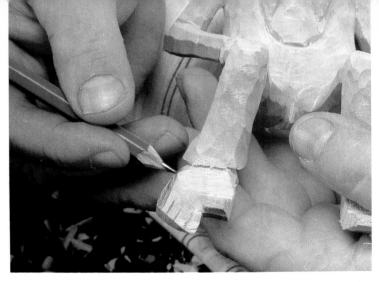

Draw in the four toes and mark any area to be removed.

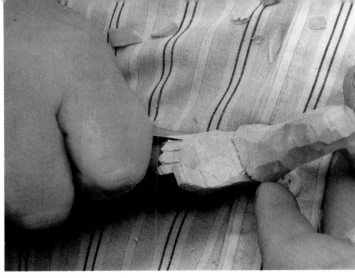

Use the same double cut on the lines between the toes.

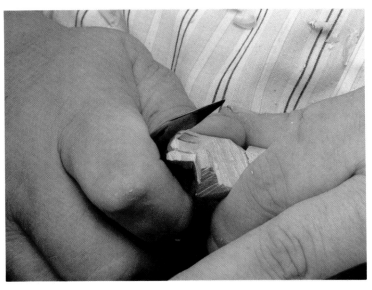

Remove the darkened area and make a notch in the ends of the toes, first cutting one way...

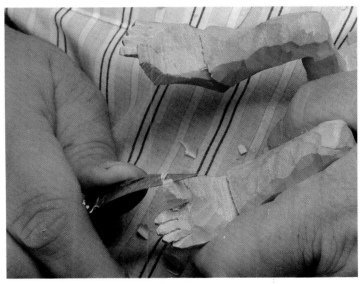

Round the big toes.

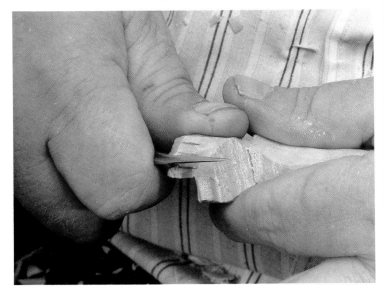

then the other.

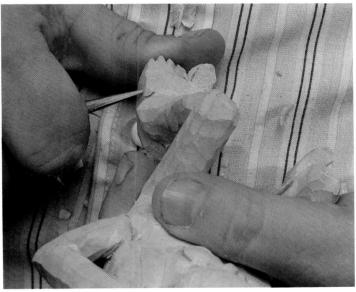

Refine the foot.

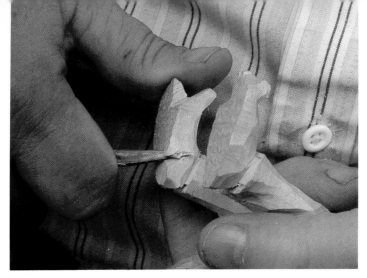

Create an arch with two cuts, one from the back...

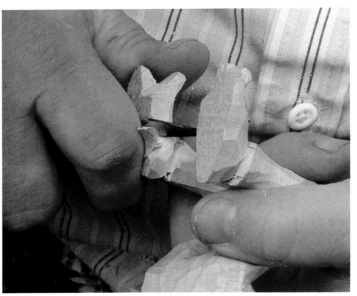

and one from the front.

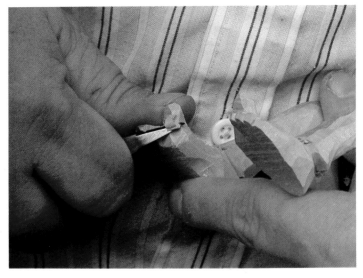

Shape the big toe with a scoop cut from the foot forward (with the grain).

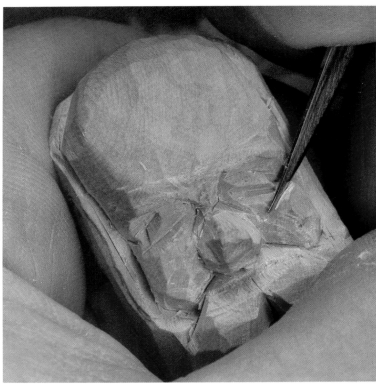

Returning to the face I want to give the eyes more character by adding some bags beneath them. This is done with double cuts...first one way...

then the other.

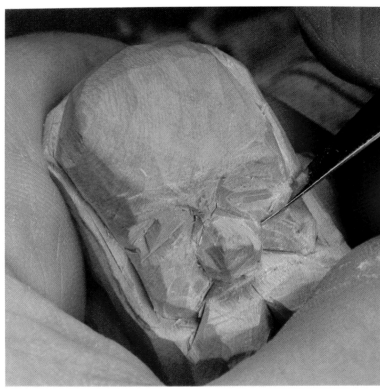

The result.

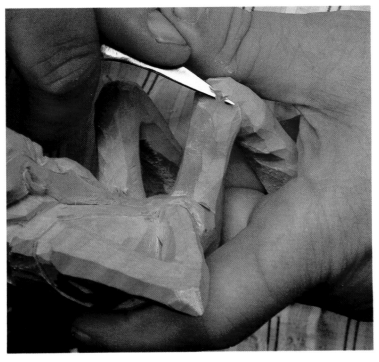

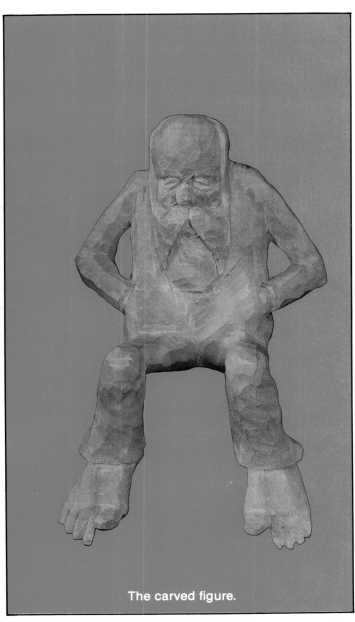

The carved figure.

Go over the whole piece, taking off saw marks, bad places, high spots, and breaking up long lines like this one on the leg.

More views of the reclining man.

Gallery of Carvings

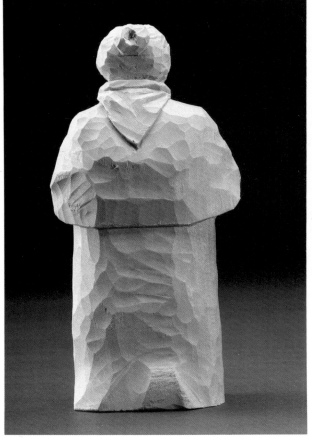

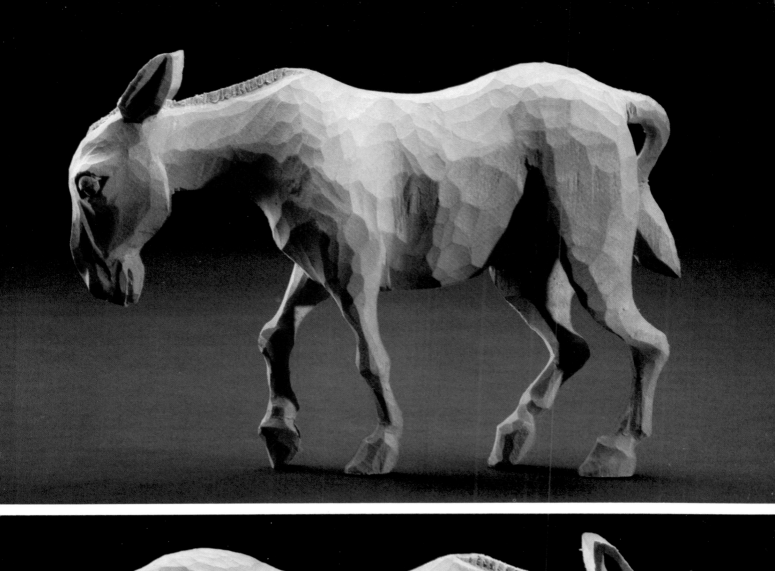

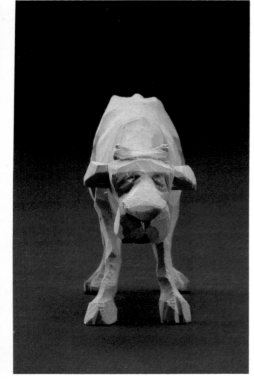

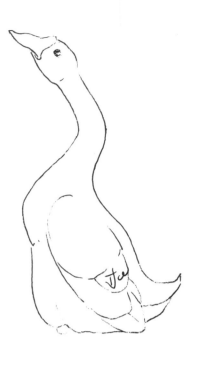

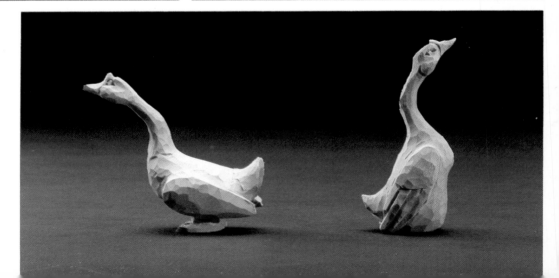